Saturday Morning Coffee with Queens

Kimberly Dixon Carroll

SATURDAY MORNING COFFEE WITH QUEENS
Copyright © 2019 by Kimberly Dixon Carroll

All rights reserved. No part of this book may be reproduced or transmitted in any form or by any means without written permission from the author.

ISBN: 978-1-7339413-5-8

Printed in USA by Vision to Fruition Publishing House (www.vision-fruition.com.com)

Photo Credits

THE PHOTOS AND the book cover were purchased from Dreamstime.com. I want to acknowledge the following photographers for their work:

Book Cover	Dreamstime
Our World	Sarah Nicholl
Fragrance of Peace	Peter Zaharov
Peace in the Heart	Joker Production
Our Future	Frederick Fahraeus
Loving Ourselves	Anthony Tiplyashin
To Know Love	Monkey Business
Organically Grown	Seesea/Dreamstime
I Am Unique	Michael Smith
Grandma	Oscar Williams
A Lesson from Grandma	Noriko Cooper
Good Night, My Love	Aiok/Dreamstime
Touched Ron	Chapple Studios
Rhythms of Love	Hasan Shaheed
Soul Mates	Andres Rodriguez
Absolute Box of Satisfaction	Raisa Kanareva
The Camping Trip	Maksym Gorpenyuk
The Music Stops	Branislav Ostojic
Does He Love Me	Onion Consultants
The Wooden Bench	Andres Rodriguez
Deception	Nikhil Gangavane
Two Loaves of Bread	Witty Verma

Table of Contents

Acknowledgments 2
The Journey for *Queens* 3
Our World 6
Fragrance of Peace 8
Peace in the Heart 10
Our Future 12
Loving Ourselves 15
To Know Love 17
Organically Grown 19
I am Unique 21
Grandma 23
A Lesson from Grandma 24
I Miss You, Grandma! 26
Good Night, My Love 28
Touched 30
Rhythms of Love 32
Soulmates 34
Absolute Box of Satisfaction 36
The Camping Trip 38
The Music Stops 41
Does He Love Me? 43
The Wooden Bench 45
Deception 47

Two Loaves of Bread 49
Addiction from the Eyes of the Non-Addicted 51
The Spiritual Will 54
The Strength to Move On 56
An Awakened Woman 59
Sweet Gratitude 62
Speak Up! 64
Happy Birthday 66
About the Author 68
About the Publisher 70

Acknowledgments

Howard Carroll, I thank you for being a supportive husband in my life. When I begin to doubt, you tell me why I can. You remind me daily of the power that God has given me to encourage others. Our love for one another is anchored in God. You are truly a blessing from God, and I appreciate you and I love you.

Heartfelt love is extended to my parents, Garland and Shirley Dixon and Dorothy Carroll; my sisters Sheretta Williams, Betina Brown, Anne Marie Sanders and Robyn Champ; my brother Roger Tatum and my cousin Michelle Leach (Cookie), all of whom at various times in my life have provided tremendous support and encouragement by their words of compassion and motivation.

Special love is expressed to my nieces Shemika Williams and Jerisa Harris and my nephew Kevin Williams. I love you all more than you know. You all are a sweet blessing to my soul.

I am grateful to all my church family at International Church of Christ who have offered so many words of encouragement, prayers and support. I am not in this life alone; and it is a blessing to have so many to hold my hand, laugh, and cry with me on my journey.

THE JOURNEY FOR QUEENS

THESE WRITINGS ARE aimed to bring hope when faced with hopelessness, bring dreams to the dreamless, and connect each reader with their own Higher Power. Women are encouraged to love themselves no matter their circumstances. Ultimately, sisters must allow themselves to speak up, define their own sense of femininity, and accept nothing less than respect.

These creative writings ruminate on peace, self-respect, domestic violence, homelessness, addiction, hurt, and love. Come take this journey for ***Queens*** that will inspire women to dance in the sun, ponder in quiet moments, understand their world, and embrace transition. My sisters, we are ***Queens***, full of confidence, power, buoyancy, vigor, courage, character, determination, and wisdom.

PEACE

OUR WORLD

Our world is not a peaceful planet. We are experiencing the War on Terrorism; then there is the war in Darfur and recently North Korea had unsuccessfully launched missiles that were capable of reaching the United States. Brutal murders are taking place in our inner cities; and drug dealers are continuing to sell illegal substances to our children, brothers, sisters, mothers, and fathers. Racism is still rearing its ugly head throughout the world.

Children, women, and men are being forced out of their homes. The neighborhoods they once knew have become street-lined condo mansions. Society has left God's children, our neighbors, hungry, naked, and homeless. We must stop judging the value of human lives based on economic condition, skin color and education. We are of one race, the human race. We have more in common with one another than our differences, which makes us wonderfully unique.

Peace is attainable if we would just see each other as family members in the human race and look beyond our physical and economic differences and embrace the similarities we share as human beings. Peace is a necessary element of life and plays a major role in how we love one another. In heaven everyone is valued, respected, and loved. There is no hierarchy of class, color, or social status. Ultimately, we are all the same. No one is better than the other. We are all children of the Almighty called to love one another as the Almighty loves us.

FRAGRANCE OF PEACE

I am angry at a foul force that has taken control over my brothers and sisters. It is evil and has the stench of decomposed flesh. It dwells like a never-ending nightmare that lurks in the nooks and crannies of our cities and towns.

I want the fragrance of peace to perfume the air so when we inhale, its aroma will change our thoughts and our behavior to exemplify the love that God has ordained us to give and receive.

When we see one another, we will not see color as a negative characteristic or a superior attribute. We will see life exploding in personalities, traits, customs, and heritages.

We will see textures, heights, widths, and traditions as beautiful bouquets radiating humanness in its purest fashion. Each petal of the bouquet creates its own unique beauty.

Come now, my precious fragrance of peace, and freshen all people. Come now, my precious fragrance of peace, and destroy the stench of violence, anger, and hatred. Blanket the people and possess all souls.

The presence of your aroma makes my heart pound with exhilaration. My adrenalin begins to soar because I know that soon peace shall inhabit our world.

PEACE IN THE HEART

We must have peace in our hearts before we can have peace in this world. Imagine if this country of freedom was also a country of peace.

We would have the light of love shining brighter than the sun in the morning or the stars and moon at night. We would not have bombs, guns, gangs, racism, prejudice, or jealousy. I could go on, but the list is far greater than the ink in my pen.

If there was peace, we would have the greatest and most powerful bond any living human being could ask for – unity. There is no peace because greed and power stand strong. These negative desires lead to self-centered emotions and thoughts.

Continue to pray.
Our day of peace is near.

OUR FUTURE

A new age has dawned. Computers are calculating faster than any human could. Error rates are down, and productivity is much more profound. Stockholders' pockets are stretching and the bottom line extending.

Programmers and computer designers are gainfully employed. But the majorities are unemployed. Tongues are distorting the truth about jobs, saying jobs are not being depleted, they are being recreated.

Two people now can do what it used to take five to do. What about the other three? Shall they go to the other company that has downsized too? Downsized because it now only takes two; capitalism depends on the employed, not the unemployed.

What is important?
Is it a corporations' bottom line? But what about the human line?
I'll say it again, what about the human line? Unfortunately, today, the human line follows the bottom line.

We are moving much too fast, placing that all mighty dollar above human good.

VINTAGE LOVE

LOVING OURSELVES

There are times when love fills our heart, and we dance through life with the rhythms that awaken our senses, so much so that we see the sun shining brightly even on cloudy days. When love is good, life is good.

As an African-American woman, I have experienced the constant negative stigmas that are force-fed daily about the various shades of our skin, the thickness of our frames, and the textures of our hair.

As women, the journey to love and be loved is difficult, but we must realize that it is not our physical characteristics that give definition to our poise; it is our inner spirits. Our physical uniqueness is an adornment given to us by our Creator, but more importantly our inner spirits are our blessings. All women are wonderfully and creatively made.

TO KNOW LOVE

What is love? I have heard through various songs, Folks' understandings and friends' experiences.

But I'm left unlearned because their love is gone. I want the love that lasts forever.

The eternal, ageless love.

I want to feel the waves of this unknown sensation.
Will it make me laugh like a baby who sees her mother? Or cry like a bride on her wedding day? Or sing with the ear pleasant vocals of a songster? Or acquire a natural high like a runner who has just taken her second breath of air?

It could be that love is an arm's reach away.
But my arms are weak from reaching and never attaining.

I want to know love in its fullest capacity – joy, peace, patience, kindness, goodness, faithfulness, gentleness, and self-control.

If love is floating among the winds, blow some my way. If love is drifting in the bodies of water, drench me until I am weighty but not suppressed.

I will cherish love like a welcomed breeze on a hot summer night, cascading through an open window.

ORGANICALLY GROWN

Quiet and mysterious.
Yet my mystery is made quite known. I'm pure.
No artificial coloring. No artificial flavors.
I am made of the purest ingredients.

Organically grown is how I am known. What you see is what you get. Except for those treasures that are for him and him alone.

Where is my challenge you say? You won't find me playing games. Games are for those who need shelter from the truth. It is the truth that I seek.

This is who I am, just little old me, organically grown!

I AM UNIQUE

Underneath my imperfect skin lies a coating of mocha brown sugar. My height is taller than the usual woman. But for every inch of me there is warmth, understanding, intelligence, and humor.

My physique demands for you to hold more and see more. Quite frankly there is more of me to love. My feet, larger than the familiar size eight, permit me to travel more and explore the hearts and minds of others.

No, I am not customary in size for a woman. Neither am I customary in depth or essence. It is not easy in a world of ordinary to be unique.

I am all you see, tall, voluptuous, warm, intelligent, bright, independent, loving, and funny. It takes a superlative shell to house all of who I am. Anything less, anything smaller or shorter would be a vessel created for another.

For I am unique. Love the uniqueness within you.

GRANDMA

She had strong aspirations like a military mission. She came to DC with strong intentions. She raised four girls and changed past traditions. Her ammunition was strong ambitions.
She envisioned her four girls to become women in leadership positions.

She despised all those racist blues on the daily news, so she made sure she had on her sturdy shoes, to diffuse what they saw on the biased tube.

Her four girls were going to be independent and strong. Nope, they were not going to just tag along. They were going to dance to their own song and prove to the biased news that they were wrong.

She knew her four girls had done no wrong.
It was society that has no sense of right and wrong. She left us with a theme song:

"Fight until there is no more civil wrong, even if it takes all life long."

A LESSON FROM GRANDMA

I grew up in very different times.
Racism and segregation tried to keep us behind.
Yet we were able to give you some quite remarkable times.

We kept our eyes open and our minds strong. Continue to remain steadfast all day long. Believe it or not, the journey is still long.

Obstacles will dwindle before long.
You will sing loudly a new theme song.
To celebrate what we knew was right all along.

I MISS YOU, GRANDMA

You are someone very special in my life.
You stimulate a vibrant wind of positive energy.
You help me see life as a colorful bouquet of flowers, each pedal and stem adding to life its own beauty.

Although you are present in my spirit each and every day, I miss you because I know you have gone away. Children love candy and miss it when it is gone.

You were so sweet to me.
I miss you now that you have passed on.
But I look forward to meeting you at each new dawn.

GOOD NIGHT, MY LOVE

May the night air bring you peace and rest. May tomorrow bring you closer to God. You are thought about each day. Your heart was good. Your mind was strong.
I visualize you standing on the highest hill with your arms raised high while the wind caresses your spirit. Good night, my love, pleasant dreams.

TOUCHED

Have you ever experienced a touch without being touched?
Have you ever been kissed without being kissed?
When he is near, the chemistry is ignitable.

I can feel his breath from a comfortable distance.
How heavenly it feels. I want to exhale so we can join hands and dance in the wind.

Each movement expressing joy, love, and acceptance of one another. Our beating hearts pound out a unique rhythm that allow our spirits to embrace each other.

His voice is always sexy.
Instead of singing me to sleep, he can talk me to sleep, but not out of boredom. His vocal cords sound like a jazzy tune on a bass guitar. My head sways from side to side as I hang on to each melody of his words. Play, baby, play!

If we could get closer, he would feel the comfort of my warmth. My temperature must be higher than 98.9 degrees. He thinks I have happy eyes. But really my eyes are inviting him to explore my mind and spirit each day more and more.

RHYTHMS OF LOVE

Go ahead, dance to the choreography in the likeness of Alvin Ailey.

With each leap, you become strong and creative, singing with the strength of Pearl Bailey.

The colorful flowing ensembles submerge your mind. You once again realign with self-redefined. Because this time, you use your own creative mind. Suddenly nothing is confined.

You hear the echoes of the familiar, the winds that Kenny G delivers, as you sit next to the Potomac River.

It feels your spirit with great ambition.
And you dance and give yourself permission,
To actualize your own cognition.

The spirit is guiding you to your own personal mission. Take hold and embrace each transition. Feel the pounding of the drums move your heart.

You finally realize, you're a wonderful piece of art.

SOULMATES

Our words are musical notes to our ears. Often, we cheer. But from time to time we see tears. We act like we have known each other for years. Actually, it is the beginning of a lifelong premiere.

No other women can capture his attention. I am his unique invention. Did I mention we are two dimensions, Living in a state of honorable conditions?

Every day is a new beginning. We just keep on grinning,
Knowing no doubt that we are among the winning.

The beating of our hearts is consolation to our souls. We work together to meet our goals, as we make our way up to the celestial north pole.

We have gone far beyond a dinner date. Now I'm telling you this without debate. We are living in our own golden state, Enjoying each other as soulmates.

ABSOLUTE BOX OF SATISFACTION

I am filled with absolute satisfaction.
All around me are precious memories of our times together. You know, those occasions when smiles covered our faces.

I see the silhouettes of long conversations that stirred up good vibrations, the chapel that was full of friends and family, that day we took hands and created true relations. God gave you to me and me to you. Now we are free from all past frustrations.

We share our thoughts and work together as a team. Even though we may get a little steamed, we always allow each other to dream.

We are independent in our thinking. Yet our commonality is not sinking.

We both have affectionate hearts that run very deep. Therefore, we both know that the other is for keeps.

I see our brown frowns.
But even when our moments are down, we never leave each other or shut down. Our love is renowned because God provided us with the crown.

Our little brown frowns never stay long to cause any harm, neither too proud to say, "I was wrong." Our life together is much too strong. Come sit with me, my mild and meek.

So, we can enjoy these precious moments that are so unique.

THE CAMPING TRIP

The sun was twinkling through the trees as the fresh air caressed her face.
The eloquent sounds of nature she embraced.

She heard the chirps of birds. It sounded like a herd.
A woodpecker tapped on a tree, waking up the hornet of honeybees.

Deer grazed through the busy woods.
Eating on the green goods.
While she walked eating on baked goods.

The leaves draped in sheets of fresh dew, complemented the morning's blue hue. This was a moment that was way overdue.

The cool night air refreshed her lungs.
She could not help but belt out three songs. And the other campers sang along.

The campsite at night was lit with a roaring, cracking fire. She immediately felt inspired. She knew that her spirit had been rewired.

It was an experience that was so very pleasant.
She would never again see herself as a peasant. She had just received the greatest present.

HEARTBREAK TEACHES WISDOM

THE MUSIC STOPS

There are times when it seems like our music stops, the dancing ceases, and each day afterward feels like a heavy rainstorm with dark clouds, thick lightning bolts, and loud thunderous roars. The rain is so heavy. Our souls gasp for air, yearning for a beautiful summer day again.

My hope is that we realize at the end of each storm we have gained momentum and strength, that we allow our experiences to move us forward to higher levels of self-esteem, self-awareness, and confidence.

Daily we continue our journey where we shall embody the qualities of confidence, power, buoyancy, vigor, courage, character, determination, and wisdom. We will stand vertical knowing who we are and how we should be loved.

DOES HE LOVE ME?

Does he hold your hand in high fashion?
Does he allow you to grow and pursue your personal goals?
Does he affirm your ambitions?
Does he work with you and not against you?
Does he use words that uplift and move you into the future?
Does he greet you with a smile or a distorted face?
Do you live in an environment of joy or frustration?
Does he challenge you intellectually?
Is he patient as you experience errors as humans do?
Does he plan special moments just to see you smile once more?
Does he care for you when you are sick?
Can you depend on him when times are tough?
Or does he disappear and then reappear when times are bountiful and robust?
Are you smiling today?

THE WOODEN BENCH

My bench is made of the finest wood matter. People walk by and look at me as if I'm no good.

I watch to pick out the one that looks like Robin Hood.
Hey, mister, can you please spare some of your baked goods?

My clothes are little tattered.
But my spirit is no longer battered. Nor are any of my bones shattered.

I've chosen to wear my clothes a little tattered. It is better than waking up battered. I have peace on my bench made of the finest wood matter.

I put behind me the house where I was misunderstood. Each night in the dark I stood. Nothing I did was ever any good.

My cries went unheard. The tears he preferred.
I had better not say a word, mindful of what had just occurred.

The crux of the matter,
My mind is no longer scattered. My face is no longer shattered. My body is no longer battered. My teeth no longer chatter.
I have peace on my bench made of the finest wood matter.

DECEPTION

Cemented in anger, jealousy, and a fierce rage, she made herself known as she leaped out of her cage. That night she wanted to be on center stage, angry because she had only been allowed backstage.

Her tongue was like wildfire blazing fervently. Her flaming eyes made it known she was no longer going to be the uncovered stone.

She heaved out a hot, fierce fire with the thunderous sounds of an angry town crier, claiming that he was a liar.

I was left feeling numb,
As she looked at me like I was scum.
All I could think was what had he done?
I was not the one that had pulled a "fast one."

Her actions were demonic,
Letting me know that they had not been platonic. I tried to reach for any kind of healing tonic.

Left wounded and paralyzed of all my senses, I was left defenseless, to a woman that had lost all of her senses because a spouse had led her on with false intentions.

TWO LOAVES OF BREAD

She thought the man who brought her bread was the man who would lead to a marriage bed. She never stopped to think.

All she did was end up in bed.
If you had asked her, they were going to wed. If you asked him, they were just going to bed.

She thought definitely they were going to wed. The next day he brought her two loaves of bread. Before he left, he said, "I had a great time in bed." Again, she definitely thought they were going to wed.

She thought sex was the golden thread that would lead to the road of a marriage bed. She asked, "So when do we wed?"

He said, "You done lost your head. Drop dead! Just because I brought you some bread! That does not mean that we are going to wed!"

She said, "But you brought me two loaves of bread." He said, "Yea, but all I wanted was to go to bed." "Any woman that accepts only bread, could never be the woman that I would wed."

ADDICTION FROM THE EYES OF THE NON-ADDICTED

It is intoxicating, luring my lover with its devastating thrill. Then the hunt and chase begin that leads my lover downhill.

It operates on intoxicated influence.
Providing the psychological promise of false intentions. That their time together will end all inhibitions.

My lover spends wildly out of desperation. Bills go unpaid.
Another career down the drain.
No one heard the spouse's loud and anguished scream.
Because that job was once a celebrated dream.

Yet my lover continues with the obsession, selling with aggression and a faceless expression, Deceiving while at the same time inhaling,
Not caring at all about discretion.

It does not care that homes are broken.
Where it has caused so much pain, words go unspoken. Families are forced to say goodbye! Because they can no longer turn the same blind eye, with the hope that it is a phase with its numbered days.

The potency is psychological,
As it works against all forms of logic. My lover keeps running in a maze, Covered under a cloud of grey haze.

THE STORM ENDS

THE SPIRITUAL WILL

Paychecks are spent while children go without milk and honey. The landlord is knocking for his money.

So, you think you can't live without it?
Remember the years when you did not even know about it?

Inside of you is your spiritual will. It is strong just like black coffee.
It is waiting to be consumed.
Open your eyes to a new morning that is in bloom.

The sun has risen! It powers over all negative emotions.
It is strong and massive like the waves of the Atlantic Ocean. It will destroy that bad-conditioned emotion called addiction. Remember Christ's Crucifixion. You will be left with no more afflictions.

You will see life in a new light.
Like a newborn baby, fascinated by what is now cheerful and bright.

You will begin to love and assert yourself.
Because the soul that was once lost has now been found. Your Higher Power has placed you back on common ground.

With each rising sun, there is new meaning to explore. Just keep open the door. Your Higher Power is standing with you.

THE STRENGTH TO MOVE ON

I am not an animal, she remembered thinking and feeling. As the first hit descended, her body cringed with rejection. Wishing instead that it were a hug, she only wanted to be loved.

The jungle was calm now.
The lion dominated once again, roaring in the distance after treating her so wrong.

Her body is cold from fear.
But she can still feel the heat from the thunderous blows. She thought to herself, where did I go wrong?

Where is my voice? Where is my self-love?
Is it in the things I possess? That has caused so much stress?

Surely, no one could ever know.
That my soul is torn, and my self-esteem is worn. Surely this cannot continue to be the norm.

The door shut loudly, or so it seemed.
Her heart was racing from fear of being seen.
She took nothing except her little bit of self-esteem.

She rested in peace because she was no longer bound to that ugly past that had gone so wrong. Her head rested in the warmth of her hands. She knew she had done no wrong.

Her self-love rekindled.

Her voice now loud and strong.
God gave her tranquility and the strength to move on.

AN AWAKENED WOMAN

One morning I awoke, and suddenly I had matured. I was tired of loving those who did not love me back. I was tired of being patient only to get doused with unconcern. Daily I would scratch to keep burned-out candles lit. I would forsake my right to be happy to suffice someone else's happiness. I never once thought that I too merit love.

During my moment of transition, I learned that many of the challenges that I faced were because of my own decisions. Once I defined my own meaning of life and began to love myself, my life changed. I had to relearn what my environment had taught me about the beauty of a woman and the expectations of roles.

I validate my own being and provide my own definition of who I am as a woman. My beauty is focused on within which provides a powerful foundation that I can be proud to stand upon.

Once I recognized the value of my own being, my decisions mirrored the way I felt about myself. I stand up to claim my right to love, to be loved, to understand, and to be understood. Unlike before, those that surround me provide me with inspiration, positive advice, knowledge, and support. The empty relationships that were void of honesty, sincerity, solid foundation, spiritual guidance, and moral values are no more.

I affirm self-love and appreciate the simple things in life. My journey in life is to live life abundantly, to give back to my community, and to allow my Higher Power to provide direction. The most vital lesson learned is to be open to new wisdom and affirm change that will allow growth.

SWEET GRATITUDE

Just like the sun that kisses our face in the morning; just like summer rain that moisturizes our skin and caresses our senses with God's perfume of fresh morning dew, the sweet expression of gratitude filled my spirit.

Like each sunrise, the words of gratitude soothe my soul with affirmation. Like each raindrop, the words of gratitude ignite a kindle of energy and endurance. Jubilation permeates my spirit. The physical effects cannot be seen by a normal spectator. But God sees and knows my heart. There is so much joy, I am at a loss for words. But inside I am shouting, Great Spirit, here I am, use me for your glory.

Let me be a vehicle of change for those whose heads are bent because of the void of hope. Let me be a vehicle of change for those whose bodies and spirits are injured, from the torment of racism and prejudice simply because of the hue of their skin.

Let me be a vehicle of change for those whose knees are weak from the injustices of working long hours at minimum wage, instead of making a livable wage.

Let me be a vehicle of change for women who cannot see past the door of abuse and the feeling of worthlessness. Use me, Lord, to empower the powerless. Use me, Lord, to promote human justice.

SPEAK UP!

Stand up for the **WOMAN** you are. Your back should not bend.

Stand erect.

Your head should not hang low.
Hold your head up with dignity and pride.
Your smile should not be hidden behind a face of misery, anguish, suffering, or stress.

Let your wonderful smile glisten with joy and happiness. Never let anyone beat you down with words, a fist or actions. The Creator made you a WOMAN.

Wise
Optimistic
Majestic
Autonomous
Noble

HAPPY BIRTHDAY

Today a *Queen* was reborn. It is no doubt that you were chosen to grace this life because of your innate ability to coach and lead. You have triumphed over many obstacles. Yet you stand today with resilient determination and wisdom. You were chosen to be a catalyst of positive change. You embody a triumphant spirit that touches the spirits of many. Each day will reveal a new realization.

Happy birthday, beautiful and wonderful *Queen*!

About the Author

Kimberly Dixon Carroll was inspired to write this book with the prompting by the Holy Spirit. During her life experiences, it was words of encouragement that helped her to overcome challenges and reach higher levels in her life with God. The truth is that we all battle our own personal moments of self-doubt, insecurity, and discouragement; moments where we feel like giving up rather than going on. Kimberly's writings are gifts of wisdom and encouragement wrapped in words of inspiration to motivate her readers.

She searched for years for her purpose. Finally, God opened up the veil that was keeping her from seeing her divine mission in life. Kimberly's purpose is to breathe life into God's Creations with written words of wisdom and encouragement. She is grateful to God Almighty who poured into her the gift to draw people into personal relationship with God.

In life there are many roads to take. Kimberly is challenging her readers not to fear the road less traveled. It is on these roads where new inventions are created, new businesses are started, and education endeavors are achieved. Kimberly took a less traveled road to obtain her Bachelor of Science of Business Administration and her Masters of Business Administration. Kimberly attended college at night on a part-time base, while working full time to reach her goals. She was older than the average college student when she started school and when she finally reached her ultimate education goal with the Masters in Business Administration. It was a 10-year journey for Kimberly to complete both her educational goals.

Kimberly believes that it is never too late to dream and achieve. The less traveled roads are the roads the majority of people do not take and are unfamiliar, but that is not an indication that people should not travel on them. Kimberly's writings are a way to motivate and inspire people of all races and genders.

Born in Evansville, Indiana, Kimberly and her family relocated to Lanham Maryland at a very young age. Kimberly resides in Upper Marlboro, Maryland with her husband, Howard Carroll and their two, much loved fur babies, Rocky (Puggle) and Sasha (Boston Terrier).

About the Publisher

At The Vision to Fruition Publishing House, we are dedicated to helping others bring their personal, business, ministry & nonprofit visions to fruition.

Whether it's as grand as a book you want to write, a business you want to start, a conference or event you want to host, a ministry you want to launch or an organization you want to start; or as small as needing a computer repair, logo design or web design; The Vision to Fruition Publishing House will help you walk through the process and set you up for success! At The Vision to Fruition Group we don't have clients, we have Visionaries. We provide solutions to equip others to pursue their visions & dreams with reckless abandon.

We have published more than twenty-three authors, several of which were #1 Amazon Bestsellers. We would love for you to join our family of Visionaries as well!

Learn more here: www.vision-fruition.com

www.ingramcontent.com/pod-product-compliance
Lightning Source LLC
Chambersburg PA
CBHW051705090426
42736CB00013B/2557